Virtual Reality for Nonprofit Organizations

Aiding in Social Change

Table of Contents

Chapter 1. Introduction

Welcome to our fascinating Special Report: "Virtual Reality for Nonprofit Organizations: Aiding in Social Change". As unlikely companions in effecting real world change, we delve into the revolutionary union of the immersive world of Virtual Reality (VR) and the benevolent sector of nonprofit organizations. In this report, we unravel how these two seemingly disparate fields come together, creating extraordinary possibilities in driving forward social change. Told through illuminating case studies and expert insights, this compendium truly sheds light on how the power of technology can augment and even revolutionize non-profit endeavors. Prepare to be inspired, educated, and potentially invest in a whole new frontier of social change!

Chapter 2. Introduction: VR and Nonprofits Uniting for Social Change

Immersive technology like Virtual Reality (VR) is seen as a new horizon for many industries, presenting myriad opportunities to innovate and revolutionize the way we interact with our surroundings. Nonprofit organizations, in their quest to stir societal transformation, have begun to recognize the vast potential VR technology holds—paving the way for impactful, tangible change.

2.1. The Evolution of VR – From Entertainment to Socio-Economic Tool

Initial strides in VR technology were largely associated with the entertainment sphere – especially gaming. It provided an immersive, first-person perspective that altered the gaming experience, providing a 360-degree view of a digital environment. But VR's potential extended far beyond. Technology visionaries soon realized the capacity of VR to create realistic scenarios, stimulate emotions, and foster empathy–qualities that were much desired, yet mostly unplumbed, in the social sector.

Today, VR has evolved into a socio-economic tool capable of solving real world problems. Its applications have extended to fields as diverse as healthcare, where it is used for therapy and surgical training; to architecture, where it facilitates better spatial planning among architects and design professionals; and to education and training, where it provides immersive learning experiences.

In the non-profit world, VR's adoption is gradually accelerating. Prominent non-profits worldwide are harnessing this technology's power to enhance their efforts in social causes, from wildlife conservation to homelessness awareness, education, and disaster response.

2.2. VR Meets Nonprofits: An Innovative Union

The intersection between VR technology and the nonprofit sector is a significant point of revolution. A union of two diverse fields that holds the promise of delivering groundbreaking solutions affecting the world's most pressing social issues.

Nonprofit organizations thrive on emotions—they are the catalysts that drive donations, spur volunteerism, and promote advocacy. And VR, with its inherent capacity to trigger emotional responses, seamlessly syncs with this need. In a VR environment, people are not just observers but participants. They experience the situation firsthand, fostering empathy—which directly impacts their willingness to act. This makes VR an incredible storytelling tool for non-profits, one that not only offers a closer and more personal view of the issues but also prompts a call to action.

Yet another aspect where non-profits can harness the true potential of VR is its capability for virtual training or skill development. Through VR, they can simulate real-world scenarios for skills training, irrespective of geographical barriers, making it an effective tool for capacity building.

2.3. Unveiling the Power of Virtual Reality

Imagine being able to witness the impact of climate change in the Arctic without ever needing to step a foot outside your home or experiencing the hardships of underprivileged children halfway across the globe. Such is the power of VR - it breaks down geographical and temporal barriers, bringing distant and often neglected issues up close and personal. This power can be harnessed by non-profits to stir conscious awareness, prompt action, and inevitably, incite change.

VR provides a means of engagement that is both visceral and immersive, moving hearts instantly and compelling minds to action. When effectively employed, it can be an extraordinary tool for non-profits to amplify their voice, enhance their outreach, and raise more funds for their cause.

2.4. Case Studies: Nonprofits Leveraging VR

A handful of forward-thinking nonprofits have already jumped on the VR bandwagon, heralding a new era of immersive philanthropy.

UNICEF, for instance, leveraged VR to showcase the devastating effects of the Syrian crisis on children, and PETA used VR to expose the animal cruelty that goes unnoticed behind closed doors in factory farms and laboratories. Through each 'on-location' experience, viewers gain a heart-wrenching, first-hand perspective of these issues, likely stirring action.

Another brilliant example is the National Autism Society's efforts. They have employed VR to help the world understand the overwhelming sensory experiences autistic people face daily—a feat hard to accomplish through mere words or imagery.

Such cases reverberate the immense potential of VR in the non-profit sector, not just to generate funding, but more importantly, to create connections, foster empathy, and instigate action.

VR has exploded onto the scene as a powerful tool that can propel the nonprofit sector towards progress. By pairing this advanced technology with the heart of nonprofits, we're unlocking a whole new frontier for social change.

2.5. Looking Ahead: Future of VR in Nonprofits

VR's journey in the field of nonprofits has just begun. While several organizations have latched onto its potential, there's a lot more to explore and far more to achieve. As VR technology becomes more accessible and affordable, we can expect to see an uptick in its use across various other facets of nonprofit work.

In the future, we might see VR revolutionizing small grassroots organizations, enabling virtual world field trips in education-focused nonprofits, and even simulating disaster response situations for better preparedness.

Moreover, as VR and other immersive technologies refine, they will undoubtedly unlock more paths for empathy, skill-building, awareness, and driving social change.

VR and nonprofits are uniting and, in the process, reshaping the traditional dynamics of philanthropy. Through their combined power, they are effecting societal transformations, one virtual experience at a time.

These first steps into the world of VR by nonprofit organizations serve as an inspiring testament to the technology's power to drive social change. However, this is just the beginning. The potential is vast, and the journey ahead is long. This endeavor is a marathon, punctuated with innovation and adaptability, that shall continually revolutionize how the world witnesses, understands, empathizes, and ultimately, changes for the better.

Chapter 3. The Science and Magic of Virtual Reality: A Primer

To comprehend the utilization of Virtual Reality (VR) in effecting real-world change, it's imperative to understand its science and its enigma. We shall dissect its foundation, starting from its conceptualisation, and exploring its immersive experience, technical aspects, and the psychological influences it brings.

3.1. A Journey Through Time: Evolution of VR

Virtual Reality's conceptual roots can be traced back to the 1950s, with the advent of multi-sensory experiences like Morton Heilig's 'Sensorama.' This invention involved essentially a mechanical device delivering experiences - smell, sight, touch, and movements simulating a real-world scenario. Yet, the refined definition of VR that we're accustomed to today only emerged during the 1980s due to Jaron Lanier. The concept centered around replacing or supplementing perceived reality with computer-generated environments.

Notably, in 1968, Ivan Sutherland and Bob Sproull created what's generally regarded as the first VR Head-Mounted Display system (HMD), named 'The Sword of Damocles,' due to its precarious hanging structure above the user. The device offered rudimentary 3D graphics in wireframe, foretelling a future where graphical interfaces could fully engage users.

Indeed, over decades, VR has morphed from military applications and top-tier research institutions into an experience accessible to the wide public. The landmark progression came with the creation of user-friendly and cost-effective VR gear like Oculus Rift, Google Cardboard, and Samsung Gear VR. These developments have made the once-elusive VR technology a reality for the average human, kindling possibilities in real-world applications beyond gaming and entertainment.

3.2. The Technical Backbone of VR

The prime ingredient of VR is immersion, placing users in an interactive simulated environment. It's accomplished leveraging complex technical aspects. Fundamentally, VR works on a very principle of human physiology – stereoscopic vision. It's the human ability to combine two slightly different views of the world - one from each eye - into a single coherent image. VR exploits this trait through HMDs that display two slightly different images, one to each eye, thus creating an illusion of depth and solidness.

Adding to this, VR employs tracking technology to sculpt the immersive experience. It facilitates users to interact with the digital world just as they would in the real one. It's accomplished through three degrees of freedom (3DOF) or six degrees of freedom (6DOF) tracking systems. 3DOF tracks rotational movements - pitch, yaw, and roll, while 6DOF adds linear movements - forward/backward, up/down, and left/right. Such intricacy of movements adds a layer of "realness" to the virtual environment, reinforcing immersion.

Modern VR systems also leverage haptic technology that enables tactile feedback to the user, further bridging the digital-physical divide. Through VR gadgets like sensory gloves, users can 'feel' the digital world, thereby creating a more convincing and engaging simulation.

3.3. The Psychological Underpinnings of VR

While technical understanding of VR is crucial, the real magic manifests in its influence on the human psyche. As a powerful tool of illusion, VR alters our perception of reality. It's not merely about seeing the virtual world; it's about 'being' in it.

At its core, VR disregards the boundary between self and other, creating a phenomenon termed 'presence' - the subjective experience of 'being' in a non-physical world. Additionally, it fosters 'embodiment,' where users have a sense of owning and controlling a virtual body.

These experiences have profound implications. For instance, research indicates that altering an embodied avatar's appearance can impact real-life behavior, a phenomenon known as the Proteus effect. They can also induce 'virtual empathy,' where one experiences events from another's perspective, triggering empathetic responses similar to real life.

3.4. Unraveling the Magic

Together, the science and magic of VR form a potent story of human ingenuity and unravel the transformative potential of VR. Its power lies not only in simulating reality but also in creating realities that can't be accessed otherwise. While the technical groundwork of VR creates the backbone for these experiences, it's the psychological implications that truly illustrate the magic of VR.

In conclusion, VR is like an expansive canvas, limited only by imagination itself. By understanding its science and magic, we shed light on its potential, opening avenues for applications in numerous sectors that aim to drive human progress and social change, including the nonprofit world. As we move forward, it becomes crucial to explore how VR's immersive, revolutionary impact can be harnessed to catalyze change on a large scale, especially in the benevolent sector. It teases a future where technology and empathy unite, stimulating meaningful interventions and transformations. Thus, the tale of the marriage of VR and social change becomes pertinent, intriguing, and most importantly, promising.

Chapter 4. Shaping Realities: VR as a Tool for Empathy and Understanding

In an era characterized by increasing use of technology, one of the most fascinating developments has been the integration and application of Virtual Reality (VR) in the context of non-profit work. Often used in entertainment and gaming sectors, VR has found its true potential in being a conduit for fostering empathy and promoting understanding—two cornerstones of social change. In essence, it enables 'walking in another's shoes' like never before, thereby creating viscerally engaging stories that can inspire people to take action.

4.1. The Fundamentals: VR and Empathy

Our human brains are wired for stories; we respond to narratives much more than we do to cold, hard facts and statistics. Stories help us make sense of the world, understand complex issues, and perhaps most importantly, connect us with others. But what if we could take storytelling a step further than just words or even moving images? This is where VR steps in.

VR allows users to dive into the narrative wholly by stimulating the senses in an immersive experience that essentially cuts out the outside world. It makes the user an actor rather than a passive observer, making the experience personal. From a neurological perspective, when we watch something happening, the same areas in our brains light up as if we are performing the same actions. This mirror neuron effect is the basis of empathy, and VR elevates this to a new level. A user is no longer merely observing, they are living the experience.

4.2. Case Studies: VR Stirring Action Through Empathy

To better understand the power of VR in stirring empathy and propelling social action, we'll consider several impactful case studies.

In 2015, the United Nations used VR for the first time with the documentary "Clouds Over Sidra". The short film followed a 12-year-old girl living in the Zaatari Refugee Camp in Jordan. As viewers put on their VR headsets, they were immediately transported to Sidra's world. They could explore the camp, watch its people go about their day, and essentially shadow Sidra. This intimate tour of a refugee camp sparked huge empathy and understanding, directly leading to an increase in donations to the United Nations.

Elsewhere, Pencils of Promise, an organization that constructs schools in developing nations leveraged VR to transport potential donors to a rural Laos village. Through VR, they could experience firsthand the joy of students attending their new school. Witnessing the real-life impact of donations in such a vivid, visceral manner inevitably tugged at heartstrings and resulted in increased patronage.

Another impactful case to consider is Amnesty International's groundbreaking "Aleppo Street View" project. This interactive 360-degree documentary took viewers on a haunting tour of a devastated Syrian city neighborhood. The project was designed to bring attention to the human rights violations taking place and was praised for its innovation and power to inspire empathy. The project increased awareness about the situation in Syria and pushed donors and influencers to action.

4.3. Expert Insights: VR's Role in Understanding Complex Social Issues

While various case studies stand as a testament to VR's potential in promoting empathy, what do the experts say?

Researchers at Stanford University's Virtual Human Interaction Lab are studying the potential of VR to foster empathy and positive behavioral change. Early results are encouraging, with studies revealing that people who have engaged with VR simulations showing the effects of climate change, for example, are more likely to act in environmentally friendly ways afterwards.

Joshua Cohen, a researcher at the lab, has stated, "We believe VR's power comes from the sense of presence it provides. You don't just observe, you are an active participant in the event, which, research tells us, can create empathy and promote understanding."

Emily Trostel, another researcher at Stanford, stated, "Our work shows that VR can activate brain networks associated with empathy and social cognition that traditional media cannot."

4.4. Harnessing VR for Social Change: Challenges and Potentialities

Though the power of VR for eliciting empathy and understanding complex social issues is potent, it would be remiss not to mention some of the challenges. High-quality VR experiences can be expensive to create, both in terms of necessary equipment and production costs. Additionally, access to VR technology is still relatively limited, particularly in lower-income areas. This has potential to limit its reach as a tool for social justice.

However, with the cost of VR steadily decreasing and its accessibility increasing, the potential for VR to dramatically alter the way we engage with social issues is promising. By making empathy more accessible, VR is aiding in making the world more understanding and connected, bringing us all one step closer to achieving true social change. Through its power to engender empathy, VR is revolutionizing the way non-profit organizations operate, underscoring the vast potential of this new frontier in technology for social change.

In sum, VR is more than just technology: it is a tool for humanity. This is an idea that will have resounding implications for our future, as the boundaries of empathetic engagement are pushed ever further, and we find ourselves in the midst of a paradigm shift in the way we relate to and aid each other. The intersection of VR and nonprofit work therefore doesn't simply represent an insignificant blip on the radar, but rather a momentous leap forward in our collective journey towards positive social change.

Chapter 5. Fund-raising Reimagined: Virtual Reality in Action

The fundraising landscape is constantly evolving. Traditional methods, such as phone calls, door-to-door canvassing and charity events still yield results. However, as technology continues to advance, these conventional channels are being complemented with innovative and engaging tools. Among these stands out an unlikely but powerful tool: Virtual Reality. By bringing stories to life and placing donors right where the action is, VR has begun to significantly impact fundraising techniques for the better. Below, we explore abundant ways VR is shaking up the fundraising landscape.

5.1. Enthralling Storytelling and Immersive Experiences

Virtual Reality ushers in an entirely new way of telling stories. While it's crucial for nonprofit organizations to narrate the purpose of their work, the age-old practice of doing so through newsletters or press releases is no longer as effective. Instead, VR provides a fresh, immersive platform for these stories. With the ability to virtually transport people to locations across the globe or into the heart of an organization's initiatives, VR naturally stirs an emotional connection between the viewer and the cause.

In 2015, Charity: Water, a nonprofit dedicated to providing clean drinking water to people in developing countries, launched a VR campaign called "The Source". Viewers of the VR experience followed the story of a thirteen-year-old girl from Ethiopia who, thanks to Charity: Water, no longer had to make dangerous, miles-long treks for water every day. The experience struck a chord with many, including one particular fundraiser event attendee who was so moved by the girl's story that he donated $2.4 million that night.

5.2. The Expansive Reach of VR

Unlike in-person events, VR experiences are not restrained by geographical boundaries. This can significantly expand the reach of nonprofit organizations and their campaigns, granting access to international audiences otherwise unreachable. For instance, the United Nations used VR to create "Clouds Over Sidra," a film which documents the life of a 12-year-old Syrian refugee. By opening a window into the experiences of refugees, the film raised unparalleled international empathy and commitment to the cause.

In a manner similar but more extensive, Pencils of Promise, an organization aiming to increase educational opportunities in the developing world, leveraged VR to take prospective donors on a virtual tour of schools they had built in Laos. The campaign extended their geographic reach and led to visibly increased engagement and donations for the organization's mission.

5.3. VR and Data Visualization

Fundraising often comes down to convincing potential donors about the impact of their contribution. VR gives donor organizations a new way to do this, thanks to its unique capabilities in data visualization. The virtual environment can represent complex data in a digestible and engaging manner, making it easier for donors to understand the impact of their monetary investments.

For instance, data on climate change can be transformed into an immersive and visually compelling experience that clearly displays the destructive patterns of changing weather and its impacts. Such an experience not only offers data in a fresh, easy-to-understand format but also makes potential donors feel an urgency they might not from traditional presentations or written reports.

5.4. VR for Training and Simulation

Apart from presenting a cause, VR in fundraising also extends to training simulations. By providing realistic scenarios, it enables better understanding, empathy, and judgement towards the organization's mission. For example, an organization working for animal rights may develop VR simulations that immerse a user in the life of an endangered animal. Witnessing firsthand the hardships these creatures face can create a visceral connection and can be a catalyst for more generous donations.

5.5. Building Sustainable Donor Relationships

VR doesn't only work to attract new donors; it can also play a significant role in maintaining donor relationships. Regular VR updates, similar to a newsletter but more interactive, can provide donors with an immersive follow-up on how exactly their donations are being utilized and the changes they're helping bring about. Such a practice enables a level of transparency and engagement that can pave the way for long-term donor retention.

5.6. The Future of VR in Fundraising

The advent of VR in fundraising signifies a significant shift: from merely conveying data and information to generating real empathy. Its immersive nature helps donors understand the challenges faced by the beneficiaries, possibly driving more meaningful and larger contributions.

However, this nascent technology isn't without challenges. Developing a VR experience requires expert skills and can be costly.

Accessibility remains another hurdle; not every potential donor owns a VR headset. Furthermore, some find the immersive character of VR disconcerting or uncomfortable, although this is likely to change as the technology matures and becomes more mainstream.

Nonetheless, the potential benefits of VR fundraising largely overshadow these concerns. As technology develops, and more people become comfortable with it, VR could become a powerful tool, democratizing donorship and making it possible to have a real-time, in-depth connection between the donors and the causes to which they are contributing. The immersive strengths of VR could well ignite a new era of connection, empathy, and generosity in the field of fundraising.

Chapter 6. Revelatory Case Studies: Nonprofits Harnessing VR Efficacy

Virtual reality, an immersive, interactive experience produced by a computer, provides a fresh avenue for non-profit organizations to necessitate social change. This section presents several illuminating instances highlighting how nonprofits have successfully harnessed VR's potential to propagate their cause with greater conviction and persuasive power.

6.1. Bringing Home Climate Change: The United Nations Virtual Reality Project

If there's one global issue that frequently finds itself lost in translation, it's climate change. The United Nations' Virtual Reality (UNVR) project, an initiative to help global leaders better comprehend the severity of climate change, sought to bridge this gap. The UNVR project turned to virtual reality, a medium with an unparalleled ability to immerse viewers in the harsh realities of climate change.

One of the project's productions, "Clouds Over Sidra," transports viewers to the Za'atari Refugee Camp in Jordan, home to more than 80,000 Syrian refugees. The film captures the day-to-day life of a 12-year-old girl named Sidra. Users are offered an unparalleled view of what life is like in a refugee camp: children attending school, men and women going about their daily tasks, completely immersed in the narrative. This visceral experience significantly boosted the UN's efforts to secure funding for related aid campaigns, affirming virtual reality's impact in elucidating harsh realities that otherwise remain distant or abstract.

6.2. Walking the Talk about Disability: Charity: Water

A key challenge for non-profit organizations lies in convincing people of the gravity of problems they've never faced. Charity: Water, an organization focused on providing clean and safe drinking water to people in developing countries, circumvents this obstacle using virtual reality.

In "The Source," the nonprofit delivers a compelling VR experience, trailing the journey of a 13-year-old Ethiopian girl, Selam, whose life changes after her village receives a clean water source. The film encompasses scenes of Selam waking up before dawn to make her perilous trek to collect water for her family, her joy when a new clean water source is installed in her village, and the ensuing transformation in her day-to-day life.

The experience of virtually accompanying Selam on her journey has led to increased empathy and greater investment from viewers. According to Charity: Water, the VR initiative helped boost fundraising – those who viewed "The Source" were reported to donate 1.5 times more than those who had not.

6.3. Breaking the Poverty Perception: Global Nomads Group

Attempting to break the stereotypes surrounding poverty, the Global Nomads Group, an international NGO that creates interactive educational programs about global issues, used virtual reality to project an undiluted portrait of life in underprivileged regions.

Through "One World, Many Stories," users virtually travel to countries like Jordan, Afghanistan, and the Central African Republic. The program uses VR's immersive capabilities to allow viewers to experience daily life in these regions - from the lively markets to the homes of the locals. The idea is to shatter misconceptions by establishing a more human and relatable connection, thereby promoting empathy and the desire to aid in change.

6.4. Confronting Social Inequalities: Emblematic Group and Planned Parenthood

Sometimes, social change requires revealing the harsh side of the society we brush under the rug. Planned Parenthood sought out Emblematic Group, a leading immersive media company specializing in VR content, to help create a VR experience called "Across The Line." This experience centers on the abortion clinic experience, putting viewers in the shoes of those who face harassment when accessing these services.

Such visceral and immersive experiences can provide a catalytic impulse for change, triggering deeper emotional responses than standard narratives or statistics. The experience is currently used across colleges and film festivals, successfully guiding conversations around this critical health issue and influencing viewers to challenge their preconceived notions.

Through these powerful case studies, we witness VR's distinct capacity to circulate stories that may not reach audiences otherwise. These instances affirm that VR offers an innovative way to augment philanthropy, coax empathy, and inspire action, thus inciting a promising future for social change initiatives cultivated by nonprofits.

Chapter 7. From Implementation to Impact: Measuring VR Success in Nonprofits

Virtual Reality (VR) transforms the way nonprofit organizations interact with their stakeholders. The implementation of VR technology not only offers a new perspective, but it also cultivates an immersive understanding that fosters empathy and persuades action. However, just like any other investment, there needs to be a way to measure the success or impact of integrating VR into nonprofit works.

7.1. The Necessity of Quantifying Impact

Nonprofits are consistently under the microscope, especially in matters concerning financial stewardship. The nonprofit sector depends largely on public trust, hence, there is a constant need to justify expenditures and prove impact. VR, though a proven innovative tool, nevertheless represents a significant investment for nonprofit organizations. Hence, it's critical to understand the VR's success metrics.

7.2. The Framework for Measuring VR Success

An effective way to measure impact would be using a framework that factors in quantitative as well as qualitative data. Quantitative data may include metrics such as the number of VR experiences delivered, engagement rates, donations, petition signatures, and volunteer numbers. Qualitative data, on the other hand, may include subjective experience reports, changes in public perception, and policy changes influenced potentially by VR.

7.3. Case Study: Pencils of Promise

One organization that brilliantly embraced VR is Pencils of Promise. This educational nonprofit incorporated VR to take potential donors on a virtual tour of schools they support in Laos. Quantitative success was reflected in an increase in donor numbers and funds raised. Qualitative success, gauged through feedback, revealed high donor satisfaction as they 'experienced' firsthand the difference their contribution could make.

7.4. Case Study: Charity: Water

Charity: Water, known for its water projects in developing nations, collaborated with Google to create 'The Source,' a VR documentary. It not only sparked empathy but also culminated in real-time donations. The increase in donations was a clear quantitative measure of its success.

7.5. Challenges in Measuring VR Impact

Successful integration of VR and proving its worth does come with challenges. Accurately interpreting the digital metrics, justifying the cost against the outcome, and maintaining technological compatibility are some hurdles. However, these do not outweigh the tremendous potential that VR has in revolutionizing the nonprofit sector.

7.6. Pioneering New Yardsticks of Impact

VR's immersive capacity to 'show' rather than 'tell' might necessitate cultivating a new set of measurement metrics. These would need to effectively capture the visceral empathy and engagement that VR campaigns can evoke. This exploration itself represents the pioneering nature of VR in the nonprofit sector.

7.7. Conclusion

The immersion and empathy provided by VR can powerfully move people to action. Ensuring that these actions translate into measurable impacts will be key in justifying VR's ongoing use and expansion in the nonprofit sector. By grasping a clear picture of the outcomes, nonprofits can continue leveraging VR to drive meaningful social change, reaching more hearts and minds than ever before.

Creating an appropriate and comprehensive framework to gauge the impact of VR in nonprofits is currently at a nascent stage. The rapid advancements in VR technology, in conjunction with a growing appreciation for its capacity to kindle empathy, will surely lead to a more distilled understanding of how this synergy can be measured, appreciated, and enhanced in the future. VR is no longer an entity of tomorrow. It's here, and it's reshaping the nonprofit landscape in a uniquely profound and poignant manner.

Chapter 8. Breaking Barriers: Addressing the Challenge of VR Adoption

The popular perception of VR technology may veer towards entertainment, with images of gamers immersed in lifelike, three-dimensional environments often being the first that come to mind. However, the potentials of this technology surpass this limited scope and enter the realm of social action - if adopted wisely and barrier-free by non-profit organizations.

To fully leverage the capacity of VR for social change, it is crucial to address the key challenges that obstruct its mass adoption. These challenges often hinder the mainstream acceptance of VR, particularly within the non-profit sector that has traditionally been reluctant towards adopting emerging technologies.

The following sections delve into these challenges and offer insights on how to tackle them, creating an environment conducive to VR adoption in the world of nonprofits.

8.1. The Cost Factor

One of the most salient obstacles to VR adoption in the nonprofit sector lies in its perceived cost. The development of VR content can be an expensive endeavor, particularly when attempting to produce high-quality, immersive experiences. Nonprofits, especially smaller organizations with limited budgets, may find it financially challenging to invest in such technology, viewing it as a significant barrier to entry.

There are, however, several strategies to alleviate this concern. For starters, non-profits can form partnerships with tech companies willing to lend their expertise in VR technology. Several successful case studies have emerged where such collaborations have borne fruit, with non-profit organizations gaining access to high-quality VR content at a fraction of the cost.

Another approach adopted by some non-profits and charities is crowdfunding. By engaging their community and sharing their vision of how VR can contrive meaningful social changes, organizations can mobilize funds specifically dedicated to VR development.

8.2. Technological Hurdle

Another impediment to VR adoption in the non-profit sector is the technological complexity involved. Smaller organizations, in particular, might lack the technical expertise necessary to create and manage VR content effectively.

While this remains a legitimate concern, the rapid advancement of technology is simplifying VR development. There is an emerging pool of user-friendly platforms facilitating the creation of VR content without requiring an extensive background in technology.

Moreover, upskilling and reskilling current staff members or investing in digital talent can also play a crucial role in dealing with the technology hurdle. Industry-specific training programs created by AI and VR firms are enabling non-technical employees to acquire VR related skills.

8.3. Accessibility and Hardware Requirement

The requirement of high-end VR hardware constitutes another vital challenge for VR adoption, both from the perspective of the organization and the end beneficiaries. Premium VR setups often demand powerful computers and high-quality headsets - tools that may represent a significant investment.

Addressing this challenge requires the propagation of low-cost VR devices such as Google Cardboard or Oculus Go. Offering immersive experiences without requiring substantial investment, these alternatives have democratized VR access to a greater degree.

Moreover, the development of browser-based VR experiences, which bypasses the need for specific hardware, is another promising solution to address accessibility concerns.

8.4. The VR Literacy Gap

Even when the technological and financial barriers have been mitigated, the 'VR literacy gap' or a lack of understanding about the potential and operation of VR technology can still hinder its adoption. This holds true not only for the team members of non-profit organizations, but also for their donors, volunteers, and beneficiaries.

Educational initiatives, seminars and workshops can enhance VR understanding and literacy, thereby bridging this gap. In a world where digital literacy is an ever-growing necessity, filling such a knowledge gap concerning novel technologies like VR is indispensable.

8.5. Ethical apprehensions

Finally, ethical apprehensions about the use and misuse of VR also acts as a barrier. Concerns about privacy, psychological harm, and consent can result in reticence about the adoption of VR in the nonprofit sector. It is crucial that these concerns be addressed through the establishment of VR ethics guidelines and policies that safeguard users' rights.

VR adoption within the non-profit sector shouldn't be stunted by its challenges. Instead, by proactively addressing these barriers, nonprofit organizations can harness the technology's vast potential to redefine the way we engage with and drive social change. The genesis of inclusive, barrier-free adoption of VR technology indeed paints a captivating future - one where immersive, interactive experiences become instrumental in engaging people, mobilizing resources and shaping a more empathetic world.

Chapter 9. Celebrating Innovators: Spotlight on Pioneering Nonprofits in the VR Space

The first lines of the chapter bring into focus the game changers in the VR space with a non-profit motive. A revolution has begun, centered around thoughtful inclusion and creative innovation to shape the future of social change.

In this chapter, we will shine a spotlight on several innovative nonprofits which have embraced VR as a tool for raising awareness, empathy, and funds, and transformed their capabilities, challenging the traditional conventions of social good.

9.1. VR for Change: A New Paradigm in Philanthropy

Pioneering this new space within philanthropy we find the organization "VR for Change". This nonprofit sprung up with the aim to combine the immersion possibilities of VR with direct social impacts. By crafting immersive experiences that illustrate various social themes, "VR for Change" has aided donors and volunteers in understanding the realities that underprivileged individuals face daily. Their "Day as a Refugee" VR experience gave users the transformative chance to live, albeit virtually, the life of a refugee, an endeavor that garnered profound empathy, sparking decisive actions and increased donations.

9.2. Pencils of Promise: Building Virtual Schools

Next in line, we move our attention to "Pencils of Promise", an education-focused organization that harnessed VR to propel their mission further than it would have ever been using conventional methods. By building a VR experience that lets viewers tour an authentic school in rural Laos, contributors could glimpse the impact of their donations on improving education standards. The virtual tour, much more than photographs or videos, played a significant role in illustrating the gravity of the educational disparity, leading to amplified funding, volunteer engagement, and strategic partnerships.

9.3. Charity: Water: Quenching the Thirst of Reality

A notable mention on our docket of innovators is "Charity: Water". They ingeniously utilized VR to highlight the massive crisis of clean water availability in developing countries. Their VR narrative called "The Source" steered viewers through an Ethiopian woman's daily trek to fetch water, alongside the monumental change that a local clean water source meant for the community. This narrative transcended geographical distances, painting a vivid picture in the viewer's mind and successfully raising colossal funds for their mission.

9.4. Fight for Sight: A Vision in VR

A unique offshoot in our exploration of the VR realm would be "Fight for Sight". They utilised VR to simulate the visual impairments faced by millions worldwide. Through simulations imitating conditions like age-related macular degeneration or diabetic retinopathy, they aimed to foster empathy for the visually impaired. Users experiencing these simulated conditions were more likely to understand, sympathize, and donate towards the cause, proving that VR can successfully influence behavioral responses.

9.5. The Nature Conservancy: Reimagining Conservation

Likewise, The Nature Conservancy ventured into VR, creating their stunning project "This is our Future", a VR journey letting users explore the precarious future of coral reefs through climate change. By showing the direct impact of rising sea temperatures on these ecosystems, they inspired viewers to take eco-friendly actions in everyday life and prompted contributions to their conservation work.

9.6. Animals Asia: Experiencing Empathy for Animals

The collaboration between VR and animal welfare is beautifully showcased by Animals Asia. Their VR experience, "Moon Bear Rescue", emotionally engaged users, providing an immersive trip inside bear sanctuaries and conservation areas. This first-hand experience dramatically upped the number of animal welfare advocates, and consequently, boosts in donations.

Through dissecting these rather avant-garde applications of VR for social enterprise, it is clear to see that the generous intentions of nonprofits can be bolstered through technological innovation. These organizations have submerged themselves into VR and surfaced with promising outcomes that encourage others to follow suit. Their courage in venturing into new technologically-driven models unpacks an alternative reality, a reality that converges technology and benevolence, pushing for social change. With each immersive narrative, they generate a ripple in the vast seas of their respective causes, showcasing the immense potential that lies in this union of virtual reality and nonprofit work.

Stimulating both thought and action, the intertwining paths of VR and social good seem to be only at the nascent stage of their relationship. As we will ascertain in the next chapters of our journey, the future holds greater promise and endless opportunities arising from this potent partnership.

Chapter 10. Looking Ahead: Future Applications of VR in Nonprofits

Just as the introduction of standard computers and the internet has revolutionly impacted our lives, virtual reality (VR), an emerging technology, is poised to be a similar game-changer. VR offers a unique opportunity - to not just witness, but truly **experience** a different reality. This technology is no longer confined to the realms of entertainment and gaming; its potential applications are broad and rapidly expanding. No sector remains untouched, including non-profit organizations, which can harness this powerful tool to create meaningful and innovative connections with their target communities, thus propelling their mission with enhanced effectiveness.

10.1. The Driving Forces Behind VR Adoption in Nonprofits

As we move forward, it is essential to understand the drivers behind the adoption of VR by nonprofits. VR allows charities to generate empathy, involving donors in their cause in profoundly transformative ways. For instance, UNICEF's VR documentary, "Clouds Over Sidra," transports viewers into a day in the life of a 12-year-old Syrian girl living in a Jordanian refugee camp. The emotional connection fostered through this immersive experience elicits a level of empathy unparalleled in traditional media, making VR a potent fundraising tool.

Furthermore, the decreased cost of VR systems and the surge in availability of easy-to-use VR content creation platforms have diminished barriers to entry, allowing nonprofits to explore its potential. Coupled with the widespread accessibility of low-cost VR headsets such as Google Cardboard, the distribution of VR content has never been easier.

10.2. Training and Skill Development

Nonprofits often function within limited budgets, requiring innovative solutions to train their staff and volunteers. VR provides an immersive, interactive environment for real-world simulations, making it ideal for training purposes. It offers a safe space to learn, make mistakes, and acquire new skills without real-world consequences. This ability to infinitely recreate and rehearse scenarios can be especially beneficial when training for disaster response, medical emergencies, or conflict negotiation.

Looking ahead, VR technology may become a staple in nonprofit training programs. Its potential to simulate complex, risk-laden situations makes it an invaluable tool for nonprofits dealing with crisis response, public safety, health services, and more.

10.3. Advocacy and Awareness

Rising above the noise to make your voice heard is a common challenge faced by nonprofits. VR's storytelling potential offers an innovative solution, enabling advocacy organizations to immerse viewers in the realities their mission seeks to overcome. For instance, VR can bring viewers face-to-face with the severe environmental consequences of deforestation or climate change, fostering a deeper understanding and commitment to eco-conservation efforts.

As VR technology becomes more mainstream, we can expect to see a heightened usage within advocacy campaigns, enabling a more profound connection between nonprofits and their audiences.

10.4. Accessibility of Education

Nonprofits aiming to bridge the educational divide can benefit immensely from the adaptive learning environment presented by VR. Research has shown VR's effectiveness in improving retention and engagement, especially in STEM subjects, making it a promising tool for educational nonprofits.

Future developments in this field will likely include more extensive digital classrooms, opening doors for remote education access, particularly for learners located in areas with limited educational resources. This advancement will democratize education by leveling the academic playing field, ensuring every child, irrespective of geographical location, is provided an equal opportunity to learn.

10.5. Therapy and Health

The use of VR in health-related nonprofits cannot be overstated. From physical therapy—where it helps with pain management and rehabilitation—to mental health—where it provides new methods for diagnosing and treating conditions like anxiety, PTDS, and phobias—VR is paving the way for innovative therapeutic interventions.

With continued advancements in VR, we are likely to witness its broader integration into health nonprofits, enhancing their ability to offer affordable, scalable, and effective treatment methods.

10.6. Fundraising

A compelling narrative has always been at the heart of successful nonprofit fundraising efforts. VR takes this a step further by allowing donors to visualize the impact of their contributions, making them active participants rather than passive contributors.

With the widespread acceptance of VR in the future, nonprofits could offer virtual philanthropy, where donors directly interact with the projects they fund—be it assisting in building a digital representation of a school in a developing country or walking alongside beneficiaries of clean water initiatives.

10.7. Challenges Ahead

Despite its enormous potential, the integration of VR into nonprofits does not come without challenges. Data privacy and ethical issues regarding immersive content need addressing. Technical, financial and personnel barriers will also have to be overcome. However, with VR's potential benefits outweighing these concerns, nonprofits would do well to plunge into this immersive reality.

In conclusion, the adoption of VR by nonprofits presents a thrilling exploration into an as-yet-untapped potential. As we venture into this brave new world, we find a realm teeming with possibilities, ready to revolutionize the influence and impact of the benevolent sector. So here's to looking ahead, into a future where VR technology amplifies the nobility and efficacy of nonprofit missions, paving the way for profound social change.

Chapter 11. Concluding Thoughts: The Transformative Potential of VR for Social Good

As our exploration through the intersection of virtual reality (VR) technology and non-profit organizations draws to a close, it's imperative to draw attention back to the overarching question: What transformative potential does VR hold for driving social change?

11.1. Identifying the Transformations

The convergence of VR and nonprofits can indeed be transformative in myriad ways. Firstly, it can stimulate empathy by taking viewers on immersive journeys. Traditional means of communication often fall short in conveying the real-life situations and struggles non-profit organizations stand against. VR has the capacity to bridge this gap, immersing users directly into the realities these organizations seek to change, sparking empathy and promoting a call to action.

11.1.1. Case Study: "Clouds Over Sidra"

UNICEF, in collaboration with VR production company Vrse.works, created the VR documentary "Clouds Over Sidra". The film documents, through the eyes of a 12-year-old Syrian refugee, life in the Zaatari Refugee camp in Jordan. The immersive, 360-degree documentary drastically changed the way donors, activists, and volunteers understood and empathized with the refugee crisis, marking a sharp increase in contributions and proactive engagements.

VR also offers a highly immersive, interactive, and compelling method for training and educating volunteers and staff members. Through virtual reconstructions of real-world scenarios, these individuals gain firsthand experience of the challenges they may encounter in the field. This has extensive implications for disaster response, healthcare, environmental awareness, human rights education, and more.

11.1.2. Case Study: "Humanitarian Response Training"

Non-profit organizations like the International Committee of the Red Cross (ICRC) have employed VR in the training of fieldworkers, recreating disaster-stricken environments virtually to provide a realistic sense of these extreme scenarios. This not only builds capacity but also boosts the efficiency and effectiveness of on-ground efforts.

11.2. Bridging the Digital Divide

However, while we bask in these revolutionary applications of VR, it's essential not to lose sight of the "digital divide" — the gulf between those who have ready access to computers and the internet, and those who do not. As non-profit organizations navigate their way through this novel technological landscape, they must remain vigilant against reinforcing or widening this divide.

A key aspect to ensuring equitable access lies in the creation of economically viable VR tech. Pioneers in the industry are working towards this aim, generating low-cost VR solutions available to wider audiences. More inclusively designed and deployed VR experiences can help democratize this transformative technology.

11.3. Future Outlook

With continual advancements in software and hardware, it is expected that VR technology will become more affordable and accessible. As this happens, not only will the scope of existing applications expand, but entirely new ways of effecting social change will certainly emerge.

Increased research into the behavioral and psychological impacts of VR can aid in creating more effective experiences, more poignant narratives, and more engaging educational resources. As more data on these fronts become available, non-profit organizations will be better equipped to harness the full potential of VR technology.

11.4. Taking the Next Step

The path to integration of VR within non-profit organizations is vast and ripe with potential, but it also presents new challenges. As an emergent field, VR requires investment in skills and equipment and the willingness to experiment and innovate. A strategic alignment with long-term objectives and careful planning will play a crucial role in ensuring the success of such ventures.

However, the promise of a more involved and empathetic global audience, improved training and education, and the ability to meet goals more effectively make the venture a promising and impactful one. The intersection of VR and the non-profit sector has the potential to reshape our understanding of social activism, volunteering, and philanthropy.

Through this exploration, it becomes evident that VR carries vast transformative potential for fostering social good. As the technology matures and becomes democratized, non-profit organizations stand to benefit greatly from embracing it.

However, it is equally important to approach this transformative potential with a critical and conscious perspective, ensuring an inclusive and equitable utilization. As we move forward, the union of VR and non-profit organizations will undoubtedly continue to illuminate exciting new frontiers in the drive for social change. Remember, the possibilities are not only endless but also inspiring!

www.ingramcontent.com/pod-product-compliance
Lightning Source LLC
LaVergne TN
LVHW051627050326
832903LV00033B/4694